S0-BFB-358

BE A NATURE DETECTIVE

Senior Authors

J. David Cooper
John J. Pikulski

Authors

Kathryn H. Au
Margarita Calderón
Jacqueline C. Comas
Marjorie Y. Lipson
J. Sabrina Mims
Susan E. Page
Sheila W. Valencia
MaryEllen Vogt

Consultants

Dolores Malcolm
Tina Saldivar
Shane Templeton

Acknowledgments appear on page Acknowledgments 1 at the back of this book.

1999 Impression

Copyright © 1997 by Houghton Mifflin Company. All rights reserved.

No part of this work may be reproduced or transmitted in any form or by any means, electronic or mechanical, including photocopying and recording, or by any information storage or retrieval system without the prior written permission of the copyright owner, unless such copying is expressly permitted by federal copyright law. With the exception of nonprofit transcription in Braille, Houghton Mifflin is not authorized to grant permission for further uses of copyrighted selections reprinted in this text without the permission of their owners as identified herein. Address requests for permission to make copies of Houghton Mifflin material to School Permissions, Houghton Mifflin Company, 222 Berkeley Street, Boston, MA 02116.

Printed in the U.S.A.   ISBN: 0-395-79507-9   56789-WC-98

INVITATIONS TO LITERACY

Houghton Mifflin Company · Boston

Atlanta · Dallas · Geneva, Illinois · Palo Alto · Princeton

BE A NATURE DETECTIVE

White Birch
Bark

Gull
Feather

Tadpoles

Animal Tracks
Written and illustrated by
Arthur Dorros

BIG BOOK PLUS

Animal Tracks
by Arthur Dorros

Table of Contents

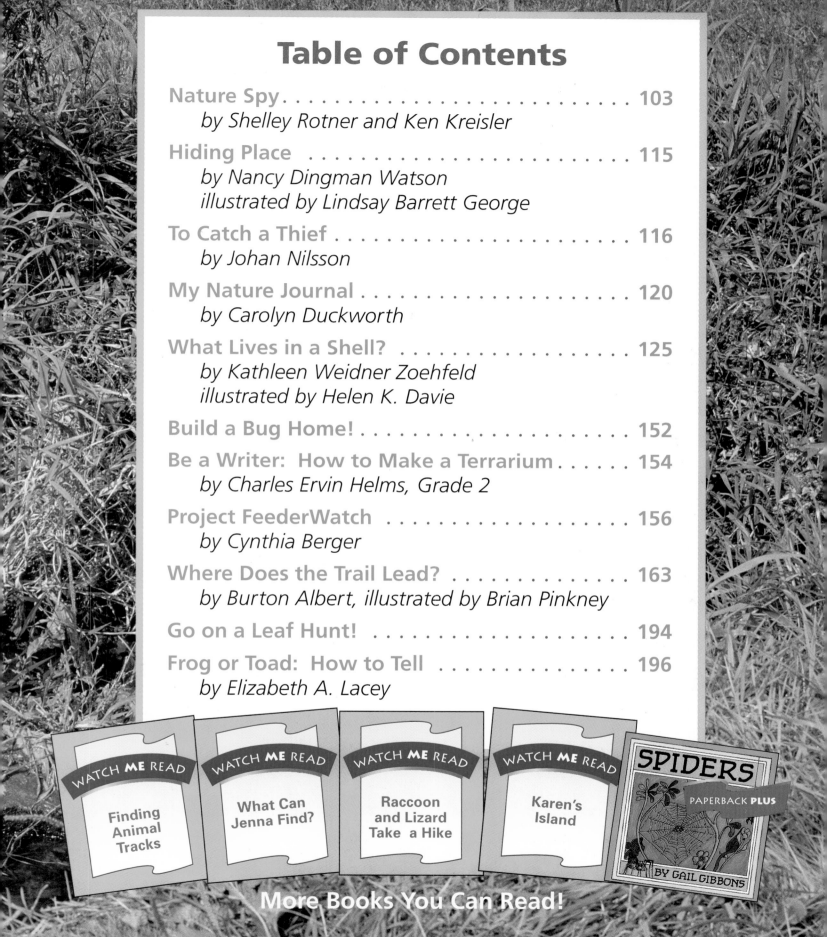

WATCH **ME** READ

Finding Animal Tracks

WATCH **ME** READ

What Can Jenna Find?

WATCH **ME** READ

Raccoon and Lizard Take a Hike

WATCH **ME** READ

Karen's Island

SPIDERS
PAPERBACK **PLUS**
BY GAIL GIBBONS

More Books You Can Read!

Meet Shelley Rotner and Ken Kreisler

Shelley Rotner didn't write children's books until she had a daughter of her own. She says, "My daughter always loved to look at books, and as she grew, I started to think and write about the subjects that interested her."

Ken Kreisler loves the outdoors. He was a United States Coast Guard captain for many years. He also worked as a fisherman.

Shelley Rotner and Ken Kreisler have also worked together on the books *Ocean Day*, *Faces*, and *Citybook*.

NATURE SPY

written by SHELLEY ROTNER and KEN KREISLER

photographs by SHELLEY ROTNER

I like to go outside — to look around and
<u>discover</u> things.

To take a really close look, even closer

and closer.

My mother says I'm a curious kid. She calls me a nature spy.

Sometimes I look so closely, I can see the lines on a shiny green leaf,

or one small acorn on a branch, or seeds in a pod.

I notice the feathers
of a bird,

or the golden eye of a frog.

When you look closely, things look
so different — like the bark of a tree or an
empty hornet's nest,

the seeds of a sunflower, or even a rock.

Sometimes there's a pattern, like ice
on a frozen pond,

or a spider's web, or a butterfly's wing.

Everything has its own shape, color, and size.
Look closely at a turtle's shell,

or a dog's fur,

or even raspberries, or kernels of corn.

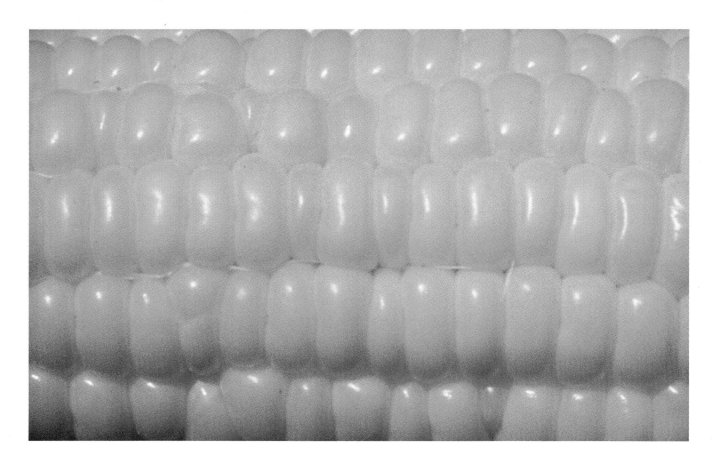

No matter where you look, up, down or all around,

there's always something to see when you're a nature spy!

Take a Closer Look

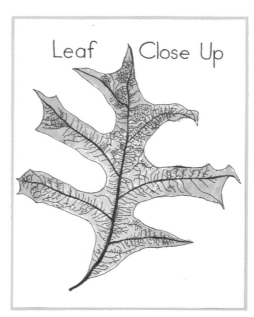

Be a nature detective like the girl in the story. Find an object, such as a leaf, a flower, or bark from a tree. Look at it up close. Draw a picture of what you see. Then draw another picture, looking at the object from far away. What did you see up close that you didn't see from far away?

Hiding Place

Down among the cobwebs, at the roots of grass
Green and creepy quiet, dewy beads of glass
Little spiders spinning, beetles bumbling through
Ants in hurry-scurries, bustling on my shoe
Tiny flowers bending when the bees weigh them down
And bouncing up fluttering the butterflies around
Down among the cobwebs and the grasshopper spittle
I can hide and peek around and be glad I am little.

by Nancy Dingman Watson

To Catch a THIEF

Ranger Rick

Dear Ranger Rick,

We had a funny thing happen in our neighborhood. Only it wasn't funny when it was happening.

I woke up one morning and went outside to sit in our yard. Soon my friend Brook woke up and came out too. (He was living with us.) When Brook got to the front porch he yelled, "Where are my shoes?" Then I realized that my shoes — my Air Jordans — were missing too! We had left them out on the porch the night before.

My Air Jordans were my favorite shoes. I was really upset. Could it be someone playing a joke, or was there a real thief out there?

That night at dinner, Brook, Mom, Dad, and I talked about the missing shoes. I thought that maybe we could make a push-button switch that would turn on when a shoe was lifted off it. Then we could catch the shoe bandit if he or she came back. My dad thought that was a great idea.

So the next day we bought a push-button switch. Once we'd figured out how to rig it up, we hooked the switch up to a spare car horn. We tried it a few times, and it worked great. Now all we had to do was wait until nighttime, and maybe we'd catch the thief.

Here's a photo of me with just some of the shoes.

Ranger Rick Magazine
8925 Leesburg Pike
Vienna, VA 22184

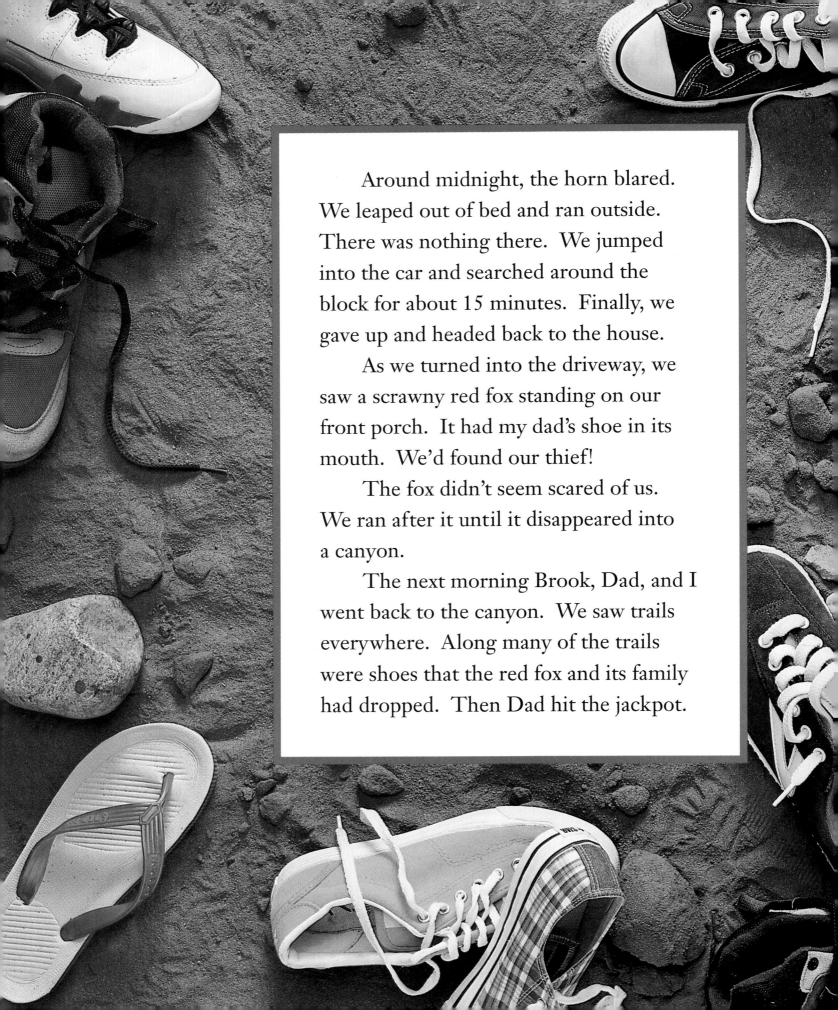

Around midnight, the horn blared. We leaped out of bed and ran outside. There was nothing there. We jumped into the car and searched around the block for about 15 minutes. Finally, we gave up and headed back to the house.

As we turned into the driveway, we saw a scrawny red fox standing on our front porch. It had my dad's shoe in its mouth. We'd found our thief!

The fox didn't seem scared of us. We ran after it until it disappeared into a canyon.

The next morning Brook, Dad, and I went back to the canyon. We saw trails everywhere. Along many of the trails were shoes that the red fox and its family had dropped. Then Dad hit the jackpot.

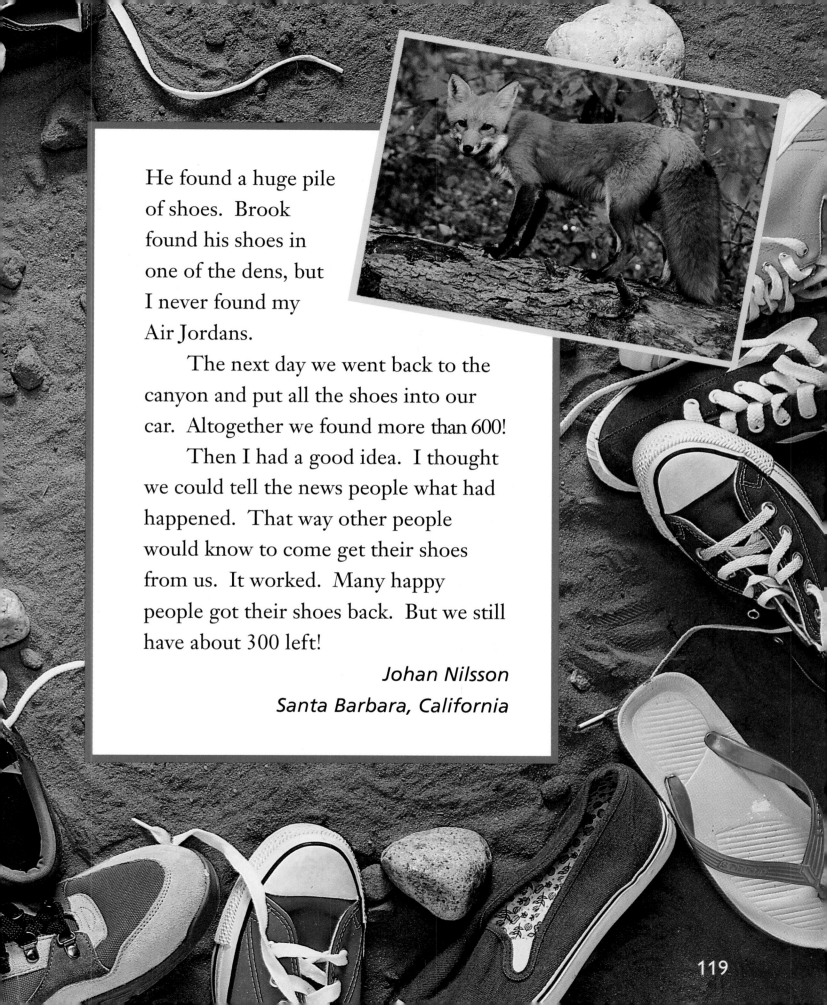

He found a huge pile of shoes. Brook found his shoes in one of the dens, but I never found my Air Jordans.

The next day we went back to the canyon and put all the shoes into our car. Altogether we found more than 600!

Then I had a good idea. I thought we could tell the news people what had happened. That way other people would know to come get their shoes from us. It worked. Many happy people got their shoes back. But we still have about 300 left!

Johan Nilsson
Santa Barbara, California

MY NATURE JOURNAL

by Carolyn Duckworth

You can keep a nature journal no matter where you are. Even if you live in a city, you can write about what you see out your window or in a city park.

WHAT YOU NEED

• **Notebook** Before you buy one, think about how you'll carry it. Will it need to fit in your pocket, a belt pack, or a back pack? Also, do you want a notebook with paper bound in or a binder you can add pages to?

• **Paper** Do you want blank paper or lined paper? It may be easier to write on lined paper, but drawings may look nicer – and be more fun – on blank paper.

• **Something to write and draw with** You can sketch with the same pen or pencil you write with and then fill in colors at home. Just be sure to write down the colors of the plant or animal that you've sketched.

HOW TO BEGIN

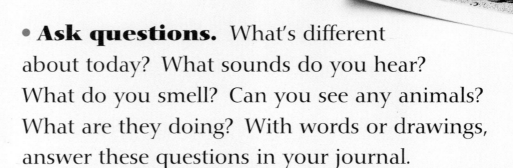

• **Go outdoors** – anywhere. Sit on your front porch, walk around the edge of a parking lot, go for a hike – just get outside! Take your notebook with you.

• **Ask questions.** What's different about today? What sounds do you hear? What do you smell? Can you see any animals? What are they doing? With words or drawings, answer these questions in your journal.

• **Show and tell.** When you draw an animal or plant, pay attention to all the details. Does it have stripes or dots on its back or head? How many petals are on the flower, and how are they arranged? Is it smaller than your little finger? Colors are important too. Finally, write down where you saw the plant or animal and exactly what it was doing.

Journal

• **Tape and glue stuff in.** Take photos and tape them into your journal. You can also tape or glue in other things, such as leaves or seeds.

Blue Jay Feather

Red Admiral Butterfly

122

• **Find that name.** At home or in the library, you may want to use a *field guide* to look up the plants and animals you've seen. If you've described the plant or animal carefully, you can often find it in a field guide – or find something that's close.

You can have a lot of fun keeping a nature journal. Hope you try it!

Peterson
First Guides®
WILD-
FLOWERS

A simplified field guide to the common wildflowers of northeastern and ... North America

Meet
Kathleen Weidner Zoehfeld

Kathleen Weidner Zoehfeld has always loved the outdoors. She grew up on a farm in the mountains, where she hiked in the woods with her father and granddad. She no longer lives in the mountains, but she still enjoys nature-watching with her family at the beach not far from her home in Connecticut.

The author with her son, Geoffrey

Meet
Helen K. Davie

Helen Davie at work in her studio. Can you find the shells?

When Helen Davie was small, her family would often go to the beach. She spent a lot of time on the shore collecting shells, since she couldn't swim that well. Ms. Davie used shells as models for her illustrations. She even kept a live snail in a jar on her desk!

124

STAGE 1

LET'S-READ-AND-FIND-OUT SCIENCE®

What Lives in a Shell?

by Kathleen Weidner Zoehfeld • illustrated by Helen K. Davie

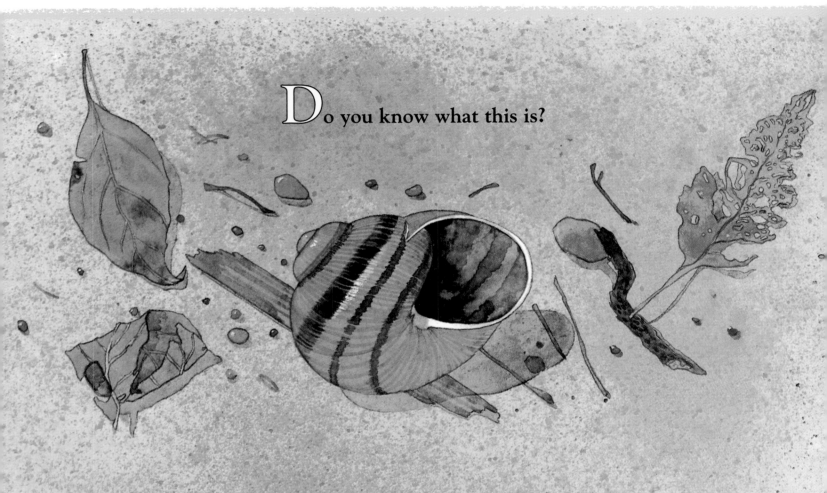

Do you know what this is?

It is as hard as a stone. But it is not a stone.
It is smooth, like glass. But it is not glass.
It is hollow inside, like a cup. But it is not a cup.
It is a shell. An animal made it. The shell was
the animal's home.

You live in a house or in an apartment building.
That is your home. Your home keeps you safe and warm.

Lots of animals have homes.
Birds build nests.

Ants make tunnels underground.

A bear likes to live in a cave.

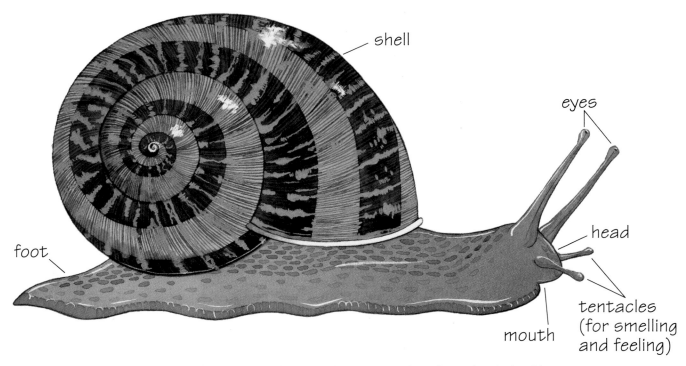

Here is the animal that lives in this kind of shell.
It is a land snail.

A land snail is born with a tiny shell. As long as
the snail lives, it keeps on growing.

As the snail grows, its shell grows with it. The
shell keeps the snail safe.

You can go in and out of your home. You can run to the playground. You can wait outside for the bus.

A snail never leaves its home. It takes its home with it wherever it goes.

The snail pokes its soft
head and its one big foot
out of the opening in its
shell. It uses its foot to inch
along. A snail is slow.

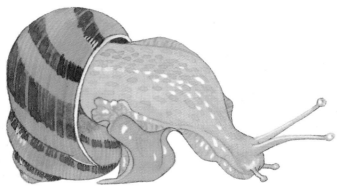

Birds like to eat snails. When a bird or other enemy comes around, a snail cannot run away. It pulls its head and foot inside its shell and closes the door. The snail is safe.

Other kinds of animals live in shells, too. Shells
come in many shapes, colors, and sizes.

Turtles live in shells. A turtle's shell can be
bumpy or smooth. Most are rounded on top and flat on
the belly.

Baby turtles have little shells. As the babies grow bigger, their shells grow bigger.

A turtle has four legs. It pokes its legs, head, and tail through the openings in its shell. Even though it has four legs, a turtle is slow.

Have you ever had a turtle race?

If a frog and a turtle were in a race, who do you think would win?

What about a cat and a turtle?

If a turtle sees a cat, it may be frightened. It may think the cat wants to eat it.

A turtle cannot run as fast as a cat. The turtle pulls its head and legs and tail into its shell. The cat pats the turtle with its paw. The turtle won't come out. It is safe in its shell home.

When you go to the seashore, you can find many different kinds of shells.

You may see a crab walking on the sand. A crab has ten legs. On its front legs are two claws. A hard shell covers its claws and the rest of its body.

A crab's shell fits it like a suit of armor. The armor helps keep the crab safe from enemies.

But just as you outgrow your favorite shirt, a crab outgrows its shell. When it gets too tight, the crab pulls itself out. Underneath is a new shell.

You may find snails buried in the sand. Some of them do not look much like the land snails.

Whelks and conchs are types of snails that are found only by the sea. Here are some different kinds of sea-snail shells.

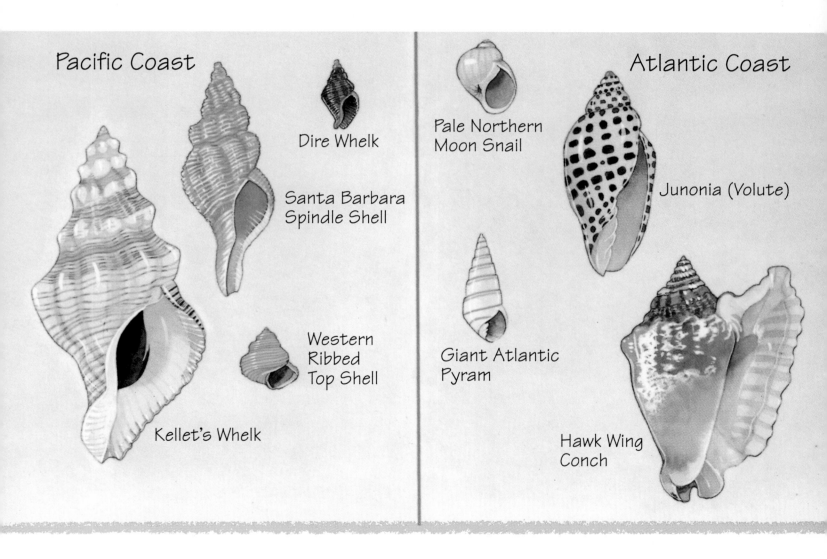

Pacific Coast

Dire Whelk

Santa Barbara
Spindle Shell

Western
Ribbed
Top Shell

Kellet's Whelk

Pale Northern
Moon Snail

Atlantic Coast

Junonia (Volute)

Giant Atlantic
Pyram

Hawk Wing
Conch

Have you ever seen a snail shell walking along on crab legs?

A hermit crab has hard claws in front, but the back end of its body has a soft shell. Its shell is too soft to keep it safe from enemies.

A hermit crab lives in an empty snail shell.

After a while the hermit crab grows too big for his shell. So he looks for a bigger one. Some are too big. Some are too small. Finally he finds one he likes. He throws away the old shell and crawls into the new one.

Now the new shell is his home. The snail shell helps keep him safe.

1

2

3

4

5

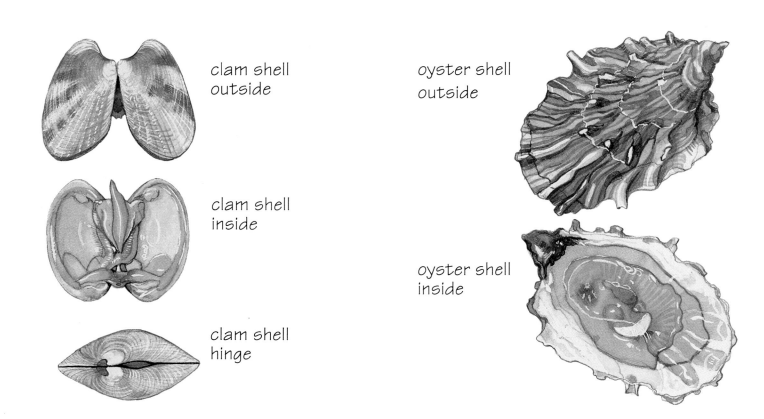

clam shell
outside

clam shell
inside

clam shell
hinge

oyster shell
outside

oyster shell
inside

You can look for clam and oyster shells at the beach, too. Clams and oysters are animals.

They have no legs. They do not have heads or tails. Their bodies are soft. But they are animals.

Clams and oysters grow two hard shells. The top shell and bottom shell look almost alike. The two shells are connected by a hinge. Scallops also have two shells. Here are some different kinds of scallop shells.

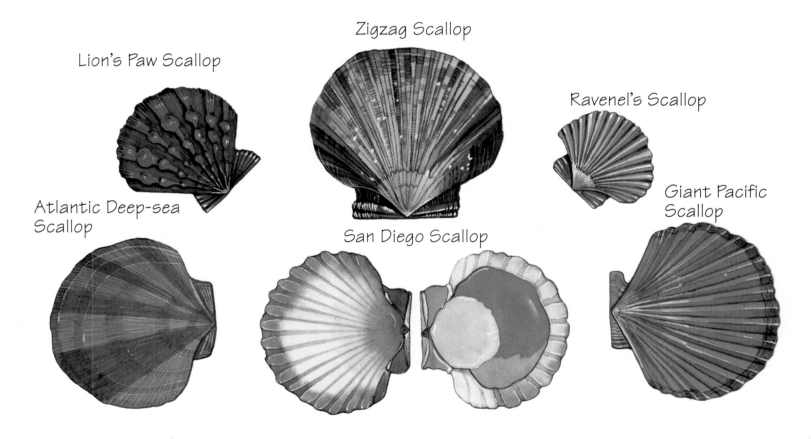

Zigzag Scallop

Lion's Paw Scallop

Ravenel's Scallop

Atlantic Deep-sea Scallop

Giant Pacific Scallop

San Diego Scallop

Most clams and oysters hardly move at all. They open up their shells to take in food and water. They close their shells tightly when enemies are around.

Some scallops can swim. A scallop does not swim like a fish, though. First it opens its two shells. Then it snaps them together quickly. This gets the scallop where it wants to go.

When you find a shell, carefully look inside.

It will probably be empty. If a shell is empty, it may mean the animal has died. Or, it has outgrown the shell and left it behind.

If the animal is at home, you can watch it for a while. See if you can tell how it eats. How does it move? What does it do when it feels frightened?

When you go, leave the animal where you found it. Animals are happiest in their natural surroundings. If a shell is empty, you can take it home with you.

If you are looking at shells in a state or national park, be sure to ask a ranger or game warden before you take any shells from the park.

Try to find as many different kinds of shells as you can. Whether the shells you find are big or small, plain or fancy — remember, a shell is someone's home.

Shell Secrets

It has legs and moves sideways.

Make shell riddles. First, fold a piece of paper in half. Then pick one of the shell animals from the story. Draw a picture of the animal on the inside of the folded paper. Write a riddle on the outside. See if a partner can answer your riddle.

Build a Bug Home!

What things make a home snug for a bug? Find out here.

— You Need —

Clear jar

Handful of soil

Rock

Leaf

Wet cotton ball

Rubber band

Piece of old stocking

Bug

1. First, put the soil in the jar. Add the rock, leaf, and wet cotton ball. How will your bug use these things?

2. Second, place your bug in the jar.

3. Next, ask a grownup to help you find out what your bug eats. Add its food to the jar.

4. Then put the stocking over the jar's opening. Use the rubber band to hold it in place.

5. Finally, watch your bug for a few days. Record what it does. Then put your bug back where you found it.

My Bug

Think about it
What things does your bug need to live? What things do you need to live?

How to Make a **Terrarium**

Instructions by Charles Ervin Helms

How do you make a terrarium? Charles wrote these instructions that tell you how he did it, step by step.

How to Make a Terrarium

This is how I made my terrarium. First, I got a jar. Then I put rocks in the bottom of the jar. Next, I went outside for sand. I put a cup of sand on top of the rocks. I poured in about one-half cup of pine chips. Next, I put a cupful of dirt in the jar. Then I planted plants and watered them. I placed my decorations, which were a gold rock and a pecan. Finally, I put on the lid. My terrarium looked wonderful!

Charles Ervin Helms

Highland Elementary School

Charlotte, North Carolina

Charles made a terrarium in second grade.
Then he wrote these instructions because he
really liked the way the terrarium turned out.
Charles also likes to swim and play ball. He
would like to be a teacher when he grows up.

155

Purple Finches

Project FeederWatch

by Cynthia Berger

Flocks of finches, colorful cardinals, and all kinds of other birds are flying to feeders at schools and in backyards. While the birds collect a meal, kids are collecting important information for scientists.

Scientists want to keep track of birds in North America. So the kids send them the information they collect. The kids are part of a program called Project FeederWatch — together with 7000 other kids and adults in the United States and Canada. The youngest FeederWatcher is five. The oldest? 91!

Sometimes we use a bird book called a *field guide* to help us find the name of a bird.

157

Our classroom is great for bird watching. With binoculars, we can see what's happening at the feeder, and we don't bother the birds while we watch them.

"We have a list of bird names, and we mark down which birds we see," says Sabrina Budny from Manorhaven School in Port Washington, New York.

FeederWatchers have to really know the birds at their feeders. They also have to be able to follow the rules for counting them.

Evening Grosbeaks

158

Cardinal

"Learning the birds' names was pretty easy," explains James Gibbons. "At first our class knew only a few. Now we can identify 23 different kinds!"

Watching Birds at School

Some kids watch feeders at home with their parents. But the kids in this story did a special FeederWatch project at several schools in New York. One thing they tried to find out was what kinds of seeds birds like best.

Birds were a part of almost every subject at our school. We weighed the bird seed as part of our math lessons. Our hungry birds ate almost 200 pounds (90 kg) of seeds last winter!

All of us kids in Project FeederWatch agreed: Working on the project was really more *fun* than work. Here we are filling a feeder with safflower seeds.

Goldfinches

Birds We Have

1.
2.
3.
4.
5.
6.
7.
8.
9.
10.

The kids used two matching feeders. One was filled with sunflower seeds and the other with safflower seeds. Every day during five-minute count periods, the kids wrote down how many birds visited each feeder. They discovered that the birds ate a lot more sunflower seeds than safflower seeds.

This winter, the school kids are testing other kinds of seeds.

We used computers to trade bird information with kids at other schools. One class only saw crows. But we had exciting news — a sharp-shinned hawk ate at our feeder.

Seen

Pine Grosbeak

Helping the Scientists

Why do scientists want the FeederWatchers to count how many birds — and what kinds — come to the feeders? One reason is that scientists want to know *where* the birds are. For example, cardinals used to live only in the southern and central parts of the United States. Now these birds are moving northward. By counting birds at feeders, FeederWatchers keep track of how different birds are spreading across North America.

Scientists also want to know if any kinds of birds are getting rare. Most feeder birds aren't in danger of becoming *extinct* (dying out). But if the FeederWatch scientists learn that some birds are getting rare, they may be able to do something quickly to help them.

Meet Burton Albert

When Burton Albert was a boy, he raised chickens and rabbits, fished for trout, and delivered newspapers. One of his first jobs as an adult was teaching school. One of his sixth grade students later became an author of children's books — just like he did!

Meet Brian Pinkney

Brian Pinkney, Age 9

Brian Pinkney says, "I make pictures for the child in me. My work is actually my way of playing." *Where Does the Trail Lead?* reminds him of his own childhood summers on Cape Cod in Massachusetts.

Where Does the Trail Lead?

By Burton Albert
Illustrated by Brian Pinkney

On Summertime Island,
where does the trail lead?
Over hills and hollows
of buttercups and snapdragons . . .

. . . to a lighthouse at the edge of the sea.

Where does the trail lead?
Past tree limbs bent by the wind,
and tide-pools of periwinkles . . .

169

. . . to gulls in flight at the edge of the sea.

Where does the trail lead?
Among families of pheasant
and rabbits in blueberries . . .

. . . to a crest of dunes
at the edge of the sea.

On Summertime Island
where does the trail lead?
Beside old tracks, grown over with grass,
where a rickety train once ran . . .

. . . to a ghost town of shanties at the edge of the sea.

Where does the trail lead?
Over the crunch of pine needles — dried and brown.
Beneath the V's and honks of geese . . .

. . . to a boat's bow of cattails at the edge of the sea.

Where does the trail lead?
Down a zig-zag of ruts from trucks in the sand.
Along railings of fence on a rocky rim . . .

. . . to the roar of surfers' waves
at the edge of the sea.

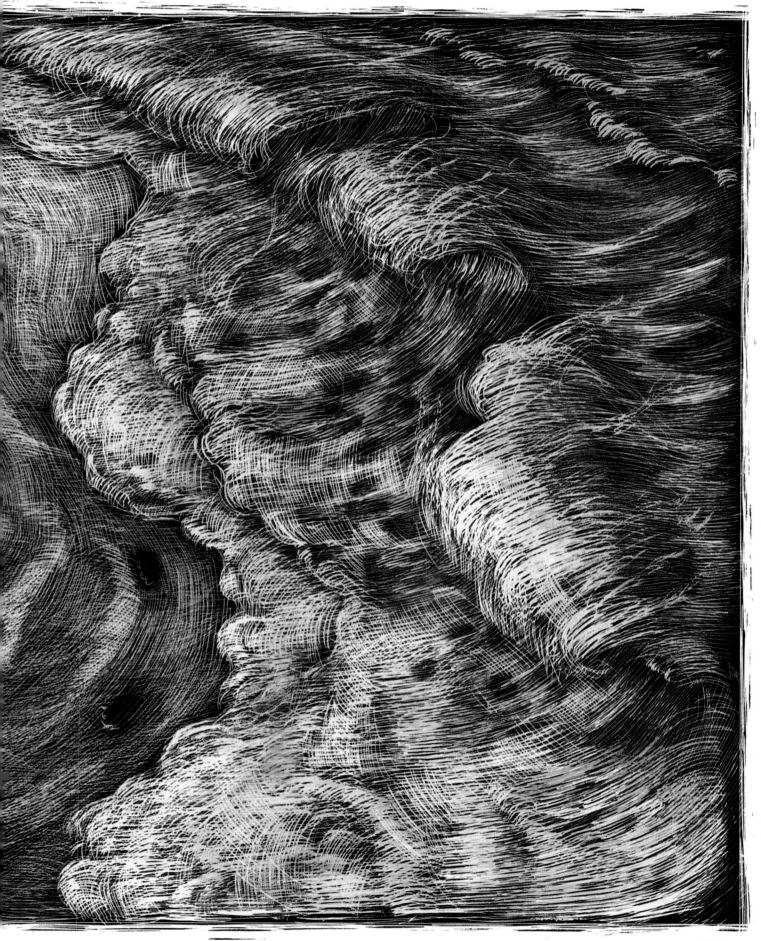

On Summertime Island,
where does the trail lead?
Back to the crackle of campfires
and the smell of fresh-caught fish . . .

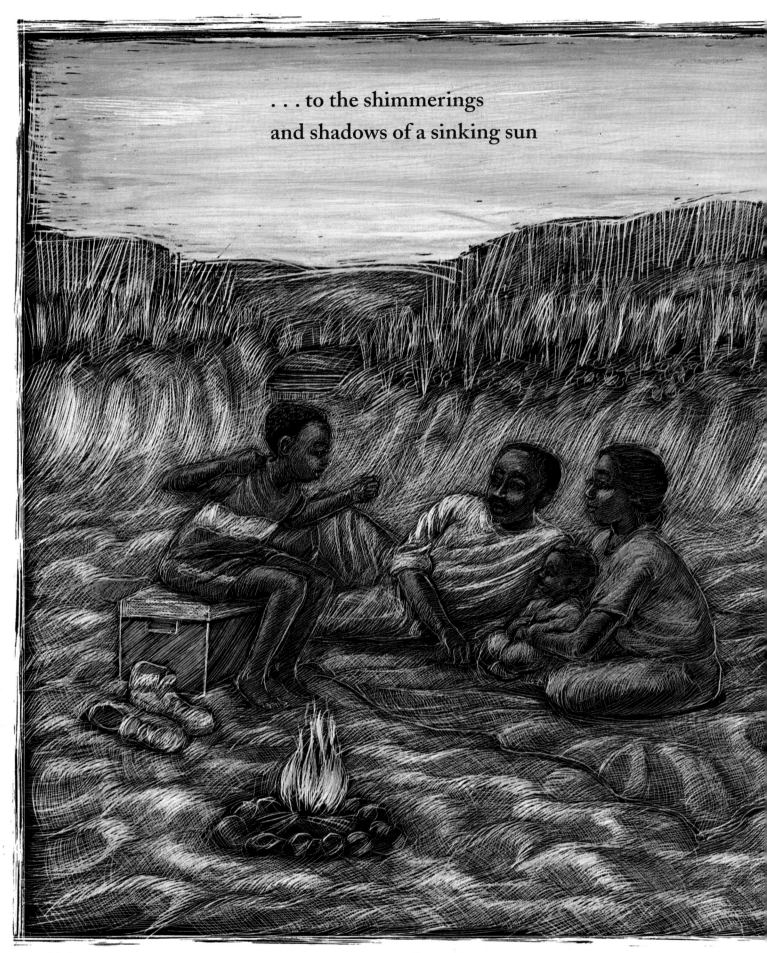

. . . to the shimmerings
and shadows of a sinking sun

in the twilight at the edge of the sea.

Adventures on Summertime Island

Think about the things you would see if you took a trip to Summertime Island. Choose a way to share your ideas.

- Make a post card to send to a friend. On the back, tell your friend about the island.

- Make a mural of Summertime Island. Draw the trail and some of the things along the trail. Work with a group or a partner.

Go on a Leaf Hunt!

Who can find the biggest leaf? The reddest one? The one most like a dinosaur? Then match your leaves with ours.

box elder

birch

scarlet oak

ginkgo

downy arrowwood

yellow oak

white oak

smooth sumac

To cock-a-doodle do the rooster, use long, feathery leaves to make its tail and neck and small leaves for its claws.

shagbark hickory

willow

bittersweet

beach pine

white pine

dogwood

blueberry

Making an animal like a mouse? Be sure to get a few leaves with long stems for its tail. And don't forget little leaves for its eyes and nose.

sassafras

195

Frog or Toad:
How to Tell
by Elizabeth A. Lacey

FROGS AND TOADS have the same overall shape and often seem much alike in color and habits. Both of these amphibians, for instance, usually lay their eggs in or near water.

Generally speaking, if you find it in a pond, it's the common frog, and if you find it in the woods, it's the common toad. But there are other clues as well.

The Common Frog	The Common Toad
Smooth, soft skin	Thick, bumpy skin
Long ridges down each side of back	Short ridges on top of head, largish bumps behind eyes
Largish round "ears" under eyes on each side	Very small round "ears" below eyes
Slender body, long legs, speedy swimmer	Plump body, shorter legs, slower moving
Lives in or very near water	Lives on land, in woods
Small teeth in upper jaw only	No teeth
Clumps of eggs laid in water	Strands of eggs laid in water
Male has eardrums larger than eyes.	Male usually has dark toes and throat.

GLOSSARY

This glossary can help you find out the meanings of some of the words in this book. The meanings given are the meanings of the words as they are used in the book. Sometimes a second meaning is also given.

A

apartment One or more rooms used as a place to live. An apartment is in a building that has groups of rooms just like it.

apartment

B

bark **1.** The sound a dog makes. **2.** The skin of a tree. Bark is thick and tough. It covers the trunk and the branches.

bark

C

claw **1.** A sharp, curved nail on an animal's foot: *The bird held on to the branch with its* ***claws.*** **2.** Part of the arm of a shellfish or an insect that can grab things: *Will the lobster use its* **claws** *to catch that fish?*

crest The top of something: *The children climbed to the* **crest** *of the hill.*

curious Wanting to learn about something very much: *Roberto asks a lot of questions because he is* **curious** *about everything.*

D

discover To learn or find out: *I discover new things about my baby sister every day.*

dune A hill of sand made by the wind: *The children ran down the sand dunes at the beach.*

dune

E

enemy A person or an animal that wants to hurt another: *A bird is the enemy of a worm.*

G

ghost town A group of empty buildings that people no longer live in: *People used to work and live in Carson City long ago, but now it is a ghost town.*

H

hinge The part of a clam or an oyster shell that holds the two halves together: *A clam opens and closes its shell by a hinge.*

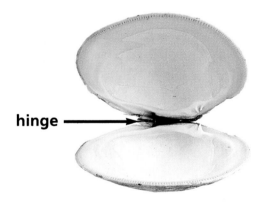

hinge

hollow Having an empty space or a hole inside: *Some animals live in hollow logs or trees.*

hornet A large wasp that stings like a bee: *If a hornet stings you, it will hurt.*

kernel A grain or a seed of a plant: *All the corn popped except for two kernels.*

lighthouse A tower with a strong light at the top that is used to guide ships away from dangerous shores: *The ship saw the lighthouse and sailed away from the rocky shore.*

lighthouse

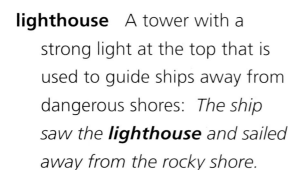

natural surroundings The place where an animal or a plant lives best or belongs. Crabs and oysters live by the oceans, which are their natural surroundings.

notice To see or hear something: *Look closely and you will notice the tiny lines on this leaf.*

opening A hole or clear space: *A turtle pulls its legs in through openings in its shell.*

outgrow To grow too big for something: *The baby will outgrow her clothes quickly.*

P

pod   The part of a plant that holds the seeds: *He had to open the **pod** to find the peas.*

pod

poke   To push forward: *My dog always **pokes** her head out the car window.*

R

rickety   Likely to break or fall apart: *Mom will fix the **rickety** old chair so we can sit on it.*

rut   A track in a dirt road made by wheels or feet: *The heavy truck left **ruts** in the road after the rain.*

S

shanty   A cabin or shack that is falling apart: *The city is going to tear down the old **shanties** and put up new houses.*

shanty

smooth   Something that feels even and has no rough spots: *My baby sister's skin feels **smooth.***

spy   Someone who watches other people or things closely to get information about them. A nature spy is someone who looks closely at plants, animals, and other living things.

suit of armor   Clothing made of metal. A long time ago, some people used armor to protect their bodies when they fought in wars.

suit of armor

T

tide-pool   Water that remains in small holes in the ground after the tide goes out: *The sea gulls are feeding on the tiny fish left behind in the* **tide-pools.**

tide-pool

track   A set of rails that trains run on: *We heard the train coming down the* **tracks.**

twilight   The time just after the sun goes down, when there is still a little light in the sky: *The stars came out just after* **twilight.**

ACKNOWLEDGMENTS

For each of the selections listed below, grateful acknowledgment is made for permission to excerpt and/or reprint original or copyrighted material as follows:

Selections

"Build a Bug Home," from *Super Science Red,* September 1994. Copyright © 1994 by Scholastic Inc. Reprinted by permission.

"Frog or Toad: How to Tell," from *The Complete Frog,* by Elizabeth A. Lacey. Copyright © 1989 by Elizabeth A. Lacey. Reprinted by permission of William Morrow & Company, Inc. Cover of March 1994 *Spider* magazine copyright © 1994 by Carus Publishing Company. Reprinted by permission of *Spider* Magazine.

"Go on a Leaf Hunt!," from "Look What I Did with a Leaf!" from October 1994 *Child* magazine. Copyright © 1993 by Morteza E. Sohi. Reprinted by permission of Walker and Company, 435 Hudson Street, New York, NY, 1-800-289-2553. All rights reserved.

"My Nature Journal," by Carolyn Duckworth. Copyright © 1994 by Carolyn Duckworth. Reprinted by permission of the author. Cover of July 1994 *Ranger Rick* magazine copyright © 1994 by The National Wildlife Federation. Reprinted by permission.

Nature Spy, by Shelley Rotner and Ken Kreisler. Text copyright © 1992 by Shelley Rotner and Ken Kreisler. Photographs copyright © 1992 by Shelley Rotner. Reprinted by permission of Macmillan Books for Young Readers, Simon & Schuster Children's Publishing division.

"Project FeederWatch," by Cynthia Berger, from December 1992 *Ranger Rick* magazine. Copyright © 1992 by The National Wildlife Federation. Reprinted by permission.

"To Catch a Thief," from November 1993 *Ranger Rick* magazine. Copyright © 1993 by The National Wildlife Federation. Reprinted by permission.

What Lives in a Shell? by Kathleen Weidner Zoehfeld, illustrated by Helen K. Davie. Text copyright © 1994 by Kathleen Weidner Zoehfeld. Illustrations copyright © 1994 by Helen K. Davie. Reprinted by permission of HarperCollins Publishers.

Where Does the Trail Lead? by Burton Albert, illustrated by Brian Pinkney. Text copyright © 1991 by Burton Albert. Illustrations copyright © 1991 by Brian Pinkney. Reprinted by permission of Simon & Schuster Children's Publishing Division.

Poetry

"Hiding Place," by Nancy Dingman Watson, from *Secret Places,* selected by Charlotte Huck, illustrated by Lindsay Barrett George. Text copyright © 1993 by Nancy Dingman Watson. Reprinted by permission of the author. Illustrations copyright © 1993 by Lindsay Barrett George. Reprinted by permission of Greenwillow Books, a division of William Morrow & Company, Inc.

Additional Acknowledgments

Special thanks to the teachers whose student's composition appears in the Be a Writer feature in this theme: Jacquelyn Peters and Kelley Valleli, Highland Elementary School, Charlotte, North Carolina.

CREDITS

Illustration 98 title by Artillery Studios **115** Lindsay Barrett George **116** title by Artillery Studios **125–150** Helen K. Davie **163–192** Brian Pinkney **196–197** Elizabeth A. Lacey

Assignment Photography Cover/Back cover Tony Scarpetta (background) **Title page** Tracey Wheeler (background); Tony Scarpetta (insets) **98–99** Tony Scarpetta **100–101** Tracey Wheeler **114** Tony Scarpetta **116–117, 118–119** Tony Scarpetta (background) **120–121** Tony Scarpetta **121** Tracey Wheeler (tr) **122–123** Tony Scarpetta **125** Banta Digital Group **151** Tony Scarpetta **152–153** Tony Scarpetta (background) **153** Tracey Wheeler (insets) **154–155** Tony Scarpetta **156** Banta Digital Group (b) **157** Banta Digital Group (tr) **158** Tony Scarpetta (tl) **159** Banta Digital Group (br); Tony Scarpetta (bl) **160** Banta Digital Group (tl) **160–161** Tony Scarpetta (background) **162–163** Tony Scarpetta (background) **193** Tracey Wheeler **Back cover insets** Tony Scarpetta (tm, m, bm); Banta Digital Group (b)

Photography 102–103 Letraset **102** © Shelley Rotner (tl); Courtesy of Ken Kreisler (br) **117** Gary Johnson (tr) **119** Stephen J. Kraseman/Photo Researchers (tr) **122** © L. West/FPG International **124** Courtesy of Kathleen Zoehfeld (t); Courtesy of Helen Davie **124–125** © Randy Faris/Westlight **152** Don Mason/The Stock Market (br) **153** Courtesy of Charles Helms (bl) **156–157** S.C. Fried/Photo Researchers (tl) **157** © Tim W. Gallagher (bl); Tom Walker (cover) **158–159** © Tim W. Gallagher **158** Stephen Krasemann/Photo Researchers (b) **159** Helen Williams/Photo Researchers; © Tim W. Gallagher (mr) **160** © Tim W. Gallagher (tl); Photo Researchers (ml) **161** © Tim W. Gallagher (tl); Stephen Kraseman/ Photo Researchers (mr) **162** Courtesy of Burton Albert (tl); Courtesy of Brian Pinkney (bl, br) **194** John Gillmoure/The Stock Market (background) **197** Tom Walker (cover) **Glossary 1** E. Bodin/Stock Boston (l); Michael Melford/The Image Bank (r) **Glossary 2** Tony Stone Images, Chicago, Inc. **Glossary 3** Harald Sund/ The Image Bank **Glossary 4** Eric Neurath/Stock Boston (l); Ron Slenzak/Westlight (r) **Glossary 5** Steve Dunwell/ The Image Bank